GRAINS

*poems
from
the
shore*

SANDRA DODGE
pei

Copyright @2019 by Sandra L. Dodge.
All rights reserved.

The south shore of Prince Edward Island is a beautiful place. These photographs and poems capture some of the joy and inspiration we have enjoyed over many summers. It is my hope that these words and pictures will remind you that God's blessings are more plentiful than the grains of sand on any shore.

Photograph by Stephen V. Munton: 11
Photograph by Kirstin J. Dodge: 19
Photographs by Sandra L. Dodge:
Cumberland Cove: front cover, 3,4,6,7,8,10,11,12, 13,14,16,17,20,21,22,23
Augustine Cove: 18, 19
Victoria: 24, 25
Tryon: 9
Cavendish: 5, 15

All photographs copyright@2019 by Sandra L. Dodge
All poems copyright@2019 by Sandra L. Dodge
Grains and Sunrise Seeker were previously published on the PEI Poet Lauriat Website
No part of this book may be reproduced in any form without written permission from the publisher.

Dedication

This book is dedicated to all our visiting friends and family.

Contents

Grains	5
Liquid Leopard Skin	7
Edges	9
Sunrise Seeker	11
Turquoise Blue Reunion	13
Going to Zellers	15
Skipping Stones	17
Hard Edge 1	19
On the Merits of Being Brave	21
The Wind Blows Wherever It Wills	23
The Lighthouse	25

ISBN: 978-0-9861987-4-8

Red Cove Publishing
www.redcovepublishing.com
peisland@gmail.com

Grains

Where does it go!
the sand that grain by grain
falls into the sea in dribs and drabs
with each tender wave kiss?

Where does it go?
Slate in slices
slakes off the red walls
which hem in the sea like a skirt.

Where does it go?
The boulder of red Island clay that
falls to its doom in the surf,
in the roar of the hurricane winds
or the silent, relentless strangle hold
of the ice bound Strait.

Does each grain and plate and rock
reappear in Cavendish –
      Resurrected White?

Liquid Leopard Skin

Red Ripples
under the surface
lunar landscape
beneath my toes
three inches of
liquid leopard skin,
the salt air in my nose.

The valleys and mountains
    of freedom
the seascape of goodness
    and love,
the light making patterns
    around my feet:
God shining down
    from above.

Each line ever changing
    in motion
each tendril of golden delight
the interplay of light
    and shadow
gives my spirit a
    smile of delight.

I'll stay in the cove
    'till the sun sets
I'll stay 'till the tide
    has gone out
I'll stay 'till the
seafloor's own ripples
echo forth with the
King's own shout.

"Well done,
good and faithful servant;
you're here at the end of
    your day.
You've seen just the skin,
meet the Leopard!
Welcome to My Shore,
    To Stay."

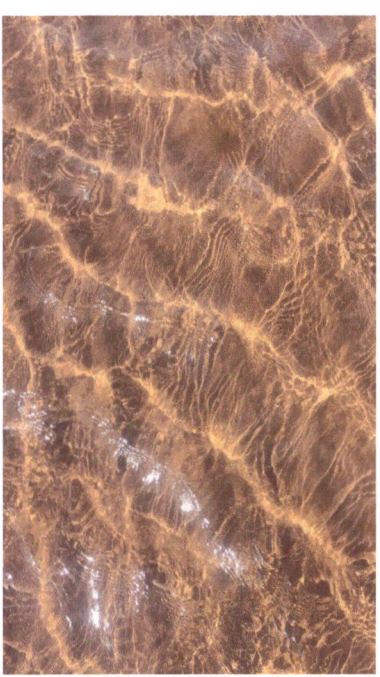

ges

ft sand

ard Soft rock

ft grass

ard soft grain

nties' lives

ard shell

ft core

EI

Sunrise Seeker

The sun slid in
   over the satin sea.
All over the cove
   the beams bounced,
barely touching the mile wide mirror,
   lightly, lofting skyward again:
undetected.

Except…

One rough craggy cliff face
presenting its pockmarked profile
   to the rising majesty,
reflected its lilting light
   in a fairy dance
all along its ragged edges.

All along its broken cheeks,
   up and down its fallen lashes,
over the whiskered boundary
      of its chin,
into the hollowed cave mouth
   never still an instant,
the fleeting, flickering
   water fairies danced,
blessing the cliff face with their
   silver iridescent ballet.

Let it be so with me, Lord.
   May I present my
fallen, broken, craggy self
   to Your Beauty:
that Your Dance of Light
   might be seen by many a
     sunrise seeker.

photo credit Stephen Munton

Turquoise Blue Reunion

Barnacle sharp sea
warm Strait welcome
foot grass gentle
golden slice of grain
cutting edge art
age old mores
best food in the house
generations meeting
four in one place
52 together, face to face
croquet conversation
fudge frosting freedom
children's laughing voices
age old music
cutting edge camp chairs
      fold and put away
      like the feelings
missing the others
five alive
five long good-byes

hard edge
      soft edge
joy at being
      together
grief at the missing
turquoise blue reunion
Island red day.

Going to Zellers

The grocery line
    winds like a slinky
into the aisle.
The cashier smiled as the black
conveyor snake slithers each item
into her grasp.
This six foot long worldwide road
moves the goods of the world
    to the consumer;
the midnight caravan across the water
coming to this consumer:
    to me
    to you
    to your grandmother
to the cousin just revisited
who came along for the ride:
going to Zellers in Summerside
goint to pick up pop,
going her own way,
putting three items
    randomly
    into the basket:
        wheat rolls
        milk
    (the staples of life)
    and the cleaner.
(cleanliness is next to Godliness, you know)

Happy outing.
Chatty
Smooth
no turmoil
just picking up a few things

until
the random items mixed
become my grocery list
and picking up a few things at Zellers
causes mushroom cloud of the stomach.

    NO!

the Cousin expletes!
grabbing her rolls

I PAY MY OWN WAY.

her pride shattered
feelings frayed
joy turned into nausea.
My grief stays with me,
it stays like gum on your shoe
like sticky paper lapels
like permanaent marker on your soul.

Even later her little barb
    "I may be poor, but…"
erodes my relational landscape
    like the tides here eat away
      at the red cliffs on the shore.
So tender
so sensitive.

If you don't know the landscape
    don't walk on the edge.
The cliff had no under pinnings
    the grass at the top was a ruse,
      and I fell.

Skipping Stones
   with Cameron and Marissa

Skip them
Skip Skip Skip
We love to skip rocks
Smells like seaweed
Looks like red, looks like blue
Rocks break
We drop rocks
They break
We chhu chhu chhu
We throw them sideways
    Chhu chhu chhu chhu
How many times can you throw them?
How many times can you skip them?
    One
        Two
            Three
                Four
                    Five
                        Six
        SEVEN!

Hard Edge

Hard edge, soft edge
water's edge
turquoise bars
red bars
sand bars
out beyond them all the rollers roll
mussel shell
clam shell
empty shell
oyster part
day's start
my heart
hears the bell,
the gong,
the whisper:
God's toll.

photo credit Kirstin Dodge

On the Merits of Being Brave

Four-year old Connor, friend Sarah
and his aloof older sister Olivia
    (she was 8)
met me on the shore.
I was the old stranger lady
    from the top of the hill.
The children followed at a
    respectful distance,
not yet sure that I could be trusted,
until, together we considered
    the cliff swallows.
I stopped moving
    and they came in closer,
        eager now to share their knowledge,
but not Olivia (she was 8).

Connor used a large stick to illustrate:
    One lived here,
Down where we stood
    at the base of the cliff.
Too low? Too large an opening?
Too scary for the bird?
Connor had certainty for answers.
No! The bravest one.
He was the bravest one, said Connor.
He was braver than the rest.
    To which there is no answer
    except a smile.

The Wind Blows Wherever It Wills

The wind blows wherever it wills
In tanglewood trills
Or Emmanuel gusts
It blows.
The wind carries scent
    of the lemon
    and cinnamon
In hot hazy days
On the brink of the rain,
On the rim of the storm plate,
The sweet smell of hope.

The wind blows wherever it wills
To the collapse of castles
    and ships
A bludgeon invisible,
The typhoon of sin,
The tempest of retribution,
The hurricaine of consequences
Brings storm wrecked debris
Blown up on His shoulder.

The wind blows wherever He wills
The baby powder blue
    of new life,
Swept in on the cool
Swept in on the fresh
Swept in, after sweeping out
Damp with the storm of repentance,
Baby powder blue on my
    windswept heart
    tearsoaked soul
Citrus scented hope.
The wind blows wherever it wills.

The Lighthouse

Deep
Buried Deep
Beneath the Stormy Sea
Are the Good times.
Deep
Buried Deep
Down there with the SeaGlass
Are the buried treasured times.
Keeper
Keeper of the good times,
Keeper of our hearts,
Keeper of our hidden pathways,
Through the storms of our lives:
Keeping watch:
    Saving, warning, guiding:
    the Lighthouse.

www.ingramcontent.com/pod-product-compliance
Lightning Source LLC
Chambersburg PA
CBHW041408160426
42811CB00103B/1548